Instant Idea Book

Instant Vocabulary Lessons

- Activities, Games, Word Lists and Word Families
  (pages 6-57)

- Reproducible Pages
  (pages 58-63)

by

Barbara Gruber

illustrations

Lynn Conklin Power

Copyright©1986 Frank Schaffer Publications, Inc.
All rights reserved - Printed in the U.S.A.
Published by **Frank Schaffer Publications, Inc.**
1028 Mirabel, Palos Verdes Estates, California 90274

ISBN #0-86734-057-6

Table of Contents

GAMES, ACTIVITIES, AND WORD FAMILIES

REPRODUCIBLE PAGES

WORD LISTS

Introduction

Instant Vocabulary Lessons provides a wide variety of activities to enhance receptive and expressive vocabulary skills. Vocabulary activities in this book complement reading, spelling, social studies and science vocabularies.

Many activities done independently by upper elementary students can be used with primary students as teacher-directed lessons. You are the expert in your classroom. Use each lesson in the way that best suits your class.

- A teacher-directed activity

- An independent student activity

- An oral pre-writing activity

- An oral and written activity on paper or the chalkboard

- An activity students do with a partner or in a small group

- A homework assignment

- Bonus or extra credit work

Your students will have fun learning new words and concepts!

Barbara Gruber

Learning New Words

Students can learn new words in many ways! Keep interest high by using this variety of student activities.

Words, Words, Words!
Write words into: sentences,
poems,
stories,
riddles,
letters,
puzzles.

Fat Cat or Chubby Feline?
List antonyms, synonyms, homonyms, or rhyming words.

Picture That!
Illustrate words.

Look It Up!
Look up definitions for words in the dictionary.

Let Me Think!
Write a list of related words.

Add It!
Add endings to root words.
(-s, -es, -ed, -er, -est)

Sort Them Out!
Classify words into categories.

FS-8307   Instant Idea Book

Learning New Words

Flashcard Flair

Students make flashcards to use at home or at school. Words are easier for students to remember if the flashcards are a unique shape. Write words that tell about electricity on cards shaped like light bulbs, or words that describe the ocean on cards shaped like seashells.

Flashcards can be used for reading, alphabetizing or sorting into categories.

(A reproducible flashcard format appears on page 60.)

Look, Remember, Write and Check

Here's a valuable activity with no papers to mark. Write a word on the chalkboard. Give students ten seconds to look at the word. Cover the word with a piece of paper while students write the word. Then remove the paper, so students can check to see if they wrote the word correctly.

I Love Puzzles

Students design crossword puzzles or word hunts on graph paper. The uniform boxes make it easy for students to print individual letters or outline crossword boxes, keeping all words/answers straight.

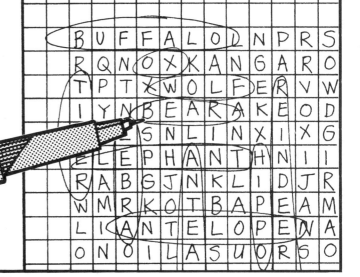

FS-8307 Instant Idea Book

Learning New Words

Buddy Drill

Assign students to a partner. Have partners test one another using flashcards.

Students play this concentration game. They write seven words on fourteen flashcards, writing each word on two cards. Students place the cards face down on a desk or table. Players take turns turning over two cards and reading the words aloud. If both cards match (are the same word), the player can pick up and keep that pair of cards. The player with the most pairs wins the game.
(Use the reproducible format on page 60 to make flashcards.)

Hunt and Peck

Give students the opportunity to type words on a typewriter.

Call a typewriter repair shop and ask if the owner would donate a typewriter to your class. Many repair shops have repaired typewriters that were not picked up by the owners. Provide a receipt, so the store can use this donation as a tax deduction.

Hear, Say, Write and Check

This is a great multi-modal approach which doesn't generate papers to correct. Say a vocabulary word aloud. Have students repeat the word aloud. Then, have students write the word and put their pencils down. Next, write the word on the chalkboard and have students check to see if they wrote the word correctly.

 FS-8307 Instant Idea Book

A Time-Saving Idea

There are several useful lists of words in this book. Instead of writing a word list on the chalkboard, consider taking a few extra minutes to print it carefully on a tagboard chart. Then, whenever you need that particular word list, simply pull out the chart. (A good way to store these charts is on a skirt hanger.)

These word lists appear in this book:

Using the Tape Recorder

The tape recorder can be used in a variety of ways in your classroom to enhance receptive and expressive language skills.

Make the tape recorder easy for young children to use. Tape a green dot of paper on the button you push for PLAY. Tape a yellow dot on the RECORD button and a red dot on the STOP button. Post directions by the tape recorder.

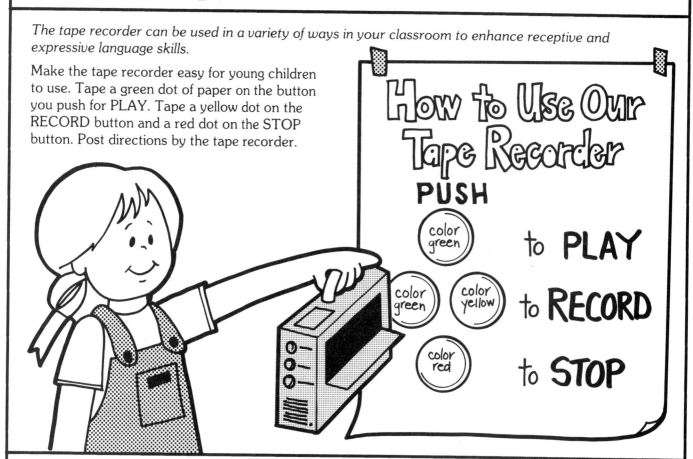

Listen-and-Read-Along Stories

You can make read-along stories during class time or use commercially-prepared book/tape sets. Place a book and its tape in an envelope with a bookmarker, so a child can follow along as the story is played.

To make read-along story tapes, select story books that you can read aloud in about ten to fifteen minutes. Read the story aloud to your class and tape record the story as you read it. Each time you read a story aloud to the class, make a tape. Before you know it, you will have a nice collection of taped stories.

FS-8307 Instant Idea Book

Using the Tape Recorder

Do-It-Yourself Vocabulary Test

Place word cards or a list of words by a tape recorder. A student can look at a word, cover the word and spell it aloud, recording it on the tape recorder. After spelling all the words aloud, the student can rewind the tape and hear himself spell the words aloud. The student can use the word list or flashcards to check for the correct spelling of the words.

My Very Own Tape

Have students bring blank cassette tapes to school. Each week write a different assignment on the chalkboard for students to record on their tapes. Why not have the girls record on their tapes one week, and the following week, give the boys a turn. Use a three-minute egg timer, so students will record for a limited amount of time.

Post a class list by the tape recorder, so students can check off their names after having a chance to record. Or, jot a list of names on the board. Students can erase their names when they have completed their turns.

Write students' names on their tapes and label side #1 and side #2. Tell students to record on #1 first.

Ideas for taping:

- Interview a friend.
- Read from your basal reader.
- Tell about a field trip.
- Tell what you like to do on Saturdays.
- Read a story or poem you wrote.
- Describe what you like best about school.
- Talk about your pet or a pet you wish you had.
- Tell about a movie shown to the class.
- Talk about your best friend.
- Describe your favorite TV show.
- Tell about a special event at school.
- Describe your favorite thing to do after school.
- Practice an oral report.

At the end of the school year, students can take their tapes home as remembrances of that year at school.

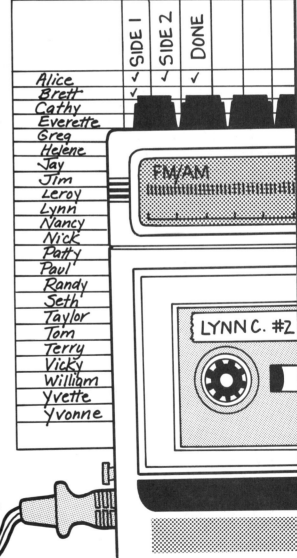

	SIDE 1	SIDE 2	DONE
Alice	✓	✓	✓
Brett	✓		
Cathy			
Everette			
Greg			
Helene			
Jay			
Jim			
Leroy			
Lynn			
Nancy			
Nick			
Patty			
Paul			
Randy			
Seth			
Taylor			
Tom			
Terry			
Vicky			
William			
Yvette			
Yvonne			

    FS-8307   Instant Idea Book

Words for the Month

Many words students learn are associated with months, holidays and seasons.

September
*school
*bus
 fall
*leaves
 rake
 brown
 orange
 red
 gold
*football
*squirrel

October
 Halloween
*pumpkin
 jack-o'-lantern
*ghost
 goblin
 costume
 mask
 Columbus Day
*ship

November
 harvest
*Pilgrim
*Indian
 Thanksgiving
 frost
 corn
*turkey
 cranberry
 thankful
*Mayflower

December
 Christmas
 Hanukkah
 holiday
*gift
 cold
 decorations
*ornament
*tree

January
 snow
 winter
 white
*snowflake
*snowman
 ice
 sled
 ski
 snowmobile

February
 red
*heart
 love
 valentine
 groundhog
 Cupid
 president

March
 green
*shamrock
 leprechaun
 lucky
 Irish
 St. Patrick
 windy
*kite

April
*umbrella
 showers
 rain
 spring
 Easter
*bunny
*chick
*lamb
*basket
 April Fool's Day
 trick

May
*flowers
*birds
 buds
 nests
 Maypole
 warm
 garden
 blossom

June
 vacation
 summer
 swim
 picnic
 play
 daylight
*sunshine
 beach
 insects
*butterfly
*boat

*Make shape-books in the form of the starred words. Students can use these books when writing stories or poems.

FS-8307   Instant Idea Book

Words for the Month

Why not provide templates and have students trace and cut out the shapes. Practice makes perfect!

Have students use the templates to cut out pieces of lined writing paper. They paste these pieces of lined writing paper on brightly colored construction paper for special handwriting practice.

Jot a word list on the chalkboard. Ask students to suggest additional words that have to do with the season, the month, colors in nature, or special holidays. For primary students, you might want to add one word to the list each day.

(See creative activities for words on pages 6 to 8.)

Monthly Extra Credit

Words of the month come in handy for extra-credit activities. Give each student a folder. List the word activities on the chalkboard beside the word list. Have students keep finished work in folders until the last school day of the month.

Today is February 3

Cupid   love
red   Valentine's Day
groundhog   February
heart

Nanci B.
Feb.
☆ Extra-Credit Folders ☆

FEBRUARY
☆ Extra Credit ☆

1. Write the words. Place this list inside your folder.

2. Write the words in ABC order. Divide them into syllables.

3. Take the extra credit spelling test.

4. Write one sentence using three words.

5. Write a poem using some of the February words.

Name Games

Teach children how to read each other's names the jiffy way!

Famous Names

Print each student's name on a flashcard. For kindergarten and first grade, use first names only. Teach students in second grade and above how to read the first and last name of each child in the class. Try covering part of the name and revealing the entire name a little at a time.

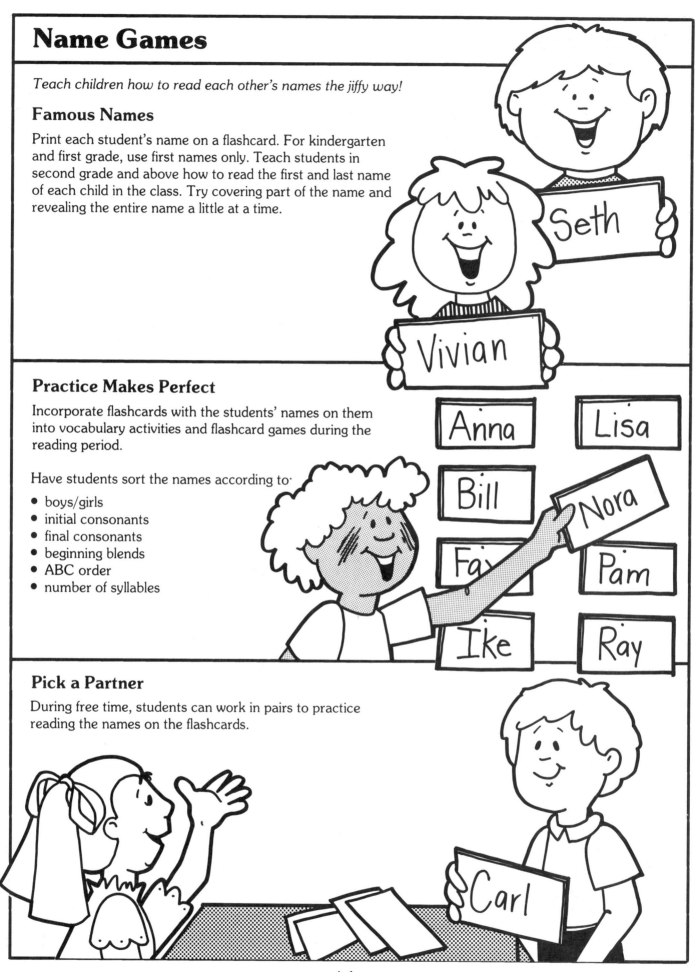

Practice Makes Perfect

Incorporate flashcards with the students' names on them into vocabulary activities and flashcard games during the reading period.

Have students sort the names according to:

- boys/girls
- initial consonants
- final consonants
- beginning blends
- ABC order
- number of syllables

Pick a Partner

During free time, students can work in pairs to practice reading the names on the flashcards.

FS-8307   Instant Idea Book

Name Games

Write Your Name

Have students print the letters of their first names vertically. Then each student writes a word or phrase about himself that begins with each letter.

Daniel
Always laughs.
Never plays on swings.
Ice cream is a favorite.
Eats lunch with Jason.
Loves to play kickball.

Kid-Proof Name Tags

Label each student's desk with his first and last name. Use a roll of clear packaging tape for a quick-and-easy way to laminate names to the desk tops.

FS-8307   Instant Idea Book

Word Families

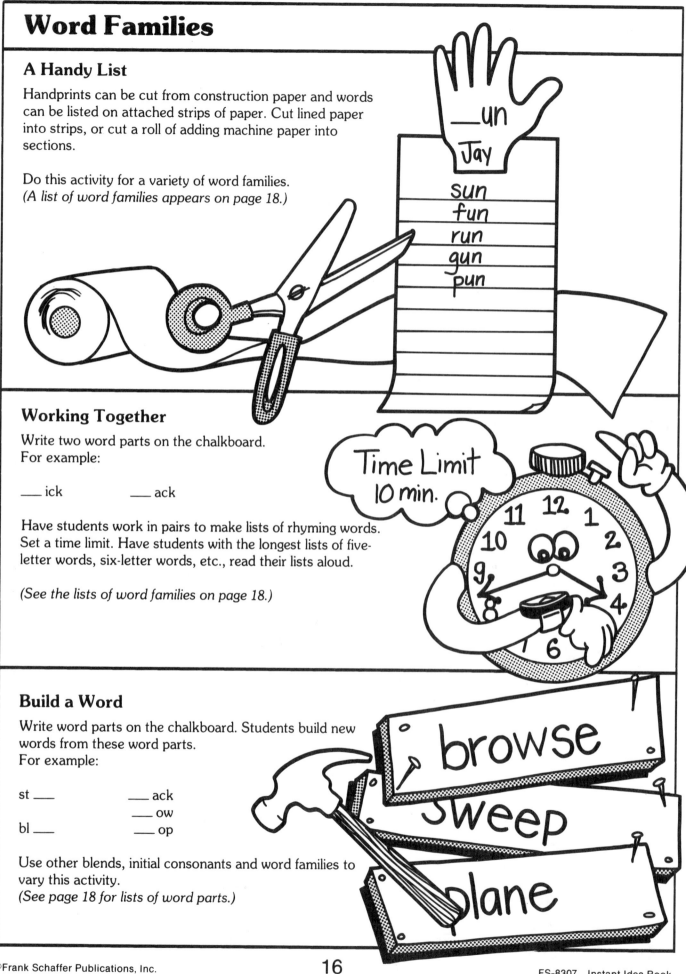

A Handy List

Handprints can be cut from construction paper and words can be listed on attached strips of paper. Cut lined paper into strips, or cut a roll of adding machine paper into sections.

Do this activity for a variety of word families.
(A list of word families appears on page 18.)

Working Together

Write two word parts on the chalkboard.
For example:

___ ick   ___ ack

Have students work in pairs to make lists of rhyming words. Set a time limit. Have students with the longest lists of five-letter words, six-letter words, etc., read their lists aloud.

(See the lists of word families on page 18.)

Build a Word

Write word parts on the chalkboard. Students build new words from these word parts.
For example:

st ___   ___ ack
                ___ ow
bl ___   ___ op

Use other blends, initial consonants and word families to vary this activity.
(See page 18 for lists of word parts.)

FS-8307   Instant Idea Book

Word Families

A Handful of Words

Write a word family you wish to introduce on the chalkboard. Have each student trace her hand on writing paper and write the word family across the palm of the outline. Students create new words by adding initial consonants or blends to each finger. Encourage students to write as many words as possible. If more than five words can be generated, have students trace their hands again and continue to list their additional words.

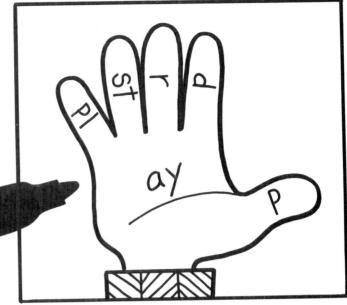

Sixteen Blends

Have students fold their papers four times, making a crease on each fold. When papers are unfolded, they will have sixteen sections.

Jot sixteen blends on the chalkboard, and have students write one blend in each section. Then give students a time limit during which they are to write one word for each blend.

After writing a word for each blend, students may write additional words in each section.

This activity also works with letter combinations found at the ends of words.
For example: -ng, -ck, -sh, -sk, -st, -gh, -rt, -rp, -ght, -ct, -ph, -lk, -nk.
(Use the list of blends that appears on page 18.)

Three-minute egg timers come in handy for this activity. Just flip the timer over at the end of three minutes for a six-minute activity.

FS-8307   Instant Idea Book

Word Families

Word Wheels

Have students make word wheels to practice word families.
(A reproducible word wheel appears on page 61.)

Reference Lists

Word Families

A		E	I	O	U	Blends
-ab	-are	-eak	-ice	-ob	-ub	bl-
-ace	-ark	-eal	-ick	-ock	-uck	br-
-ack	-ash	-eam	-id	-od	-uff	cl-
-ad	-at	-ear	-ide	-og	-ug	cr-
-ade	-ate	-eat	-ig	-oke	-um	dr-
-ag	-ave	-ed	-ight	-old	-ump	fl-
-ail	-aw	-eed	-ill	-one	-un	fr-
-ain	-ay	-eep	-im	-ong	-ung	gl-
-ake		-eet	-ime	-op	-unk	gr-
-all		-ell	-in	-ope	-ush	pl-
-am		-en	-ind	-ore	-ut	pr-
-ame		-end	-ine	-orn		sc-
-amp		-ent	-ing	-ot		sk-
-an		-est	-ink	-ow (ō)		sl-
-and		-et	-int	-ow (ou)		sm-
-ane		-ew	-ip			sn-
-ang			-it			sp-
-ank			-ive			st-
-ap			-y (ī)			sw-
-ar						tr-
						tw-

Act It Out

Students learn words quickly when they associate words with actions.

Watch Me

Make word cards containing action words for students to pantomime. Give each student a word card. Tell students not to let others see the word on their cards.

Choose a student to act out his word. That student can call on another student to guess which word the student pantomimed. After the correct word has been guessed, have all students write the word. Then, have the student who did the pantomime show his word card to the class. Students can check to make certain they spelled the word correctly.

Action Words
whistle
hum
nod
swallow
tickle
wiggle
spin
twist
yawn
push
pull
turn
scratch
pinch
tap
chew
dance
eat
stare
skip
hop
clap
wink
blink
smile
frown
wave
cry
point
jump
stamp
laugh
sing
bark
walk
run
talk
throw
catch
stretch
bend

"BLINK" "WAVE" "SING" "HOP" "TWIST" "TURN" "STAMP"

FS-8307   Instant Idea Book

A Touch of Color

Make a Rainbow

Each student selects a vocabulary word that is difficult for him to learn. Have every student print his word on a piece of paper. Words should be printed as large as possible in pencil. Have students check to make sure the word is spelled correctly.

Then students trace their words with black crayon, making a heavy black outline of each letter. Students softly say the letters aloud as the letters are traced.

Next, every student draws another outline in a different color around each letter as he spells the word aloud again. Students continue to add bands of color, so their words look like rainbows.

Like-a-Rainbow Bulletin Board

Rainbow word cards make an attractive bulletin board display. Or, you can staple papers together to make a booklet of "rainbow" words for the classroom library.

In the Spotlight!

Help students identify the trouble spots in words. Have students use highlighters or yellow crayons to trace over the letters in words that are giving them difficulty.

This highlighting technique also works well when teaching accented syllables. Have students highlight the syllables that are accented.

FS-8307   Instant Idea Book

Picture That

Make picture dictionaries to help your students gain fluency with words from a unit in reading, social studies or science.

Write the word list for your unit of study on the chalkboard.

For example:

> knight
> castle
> prince
> princess
> throne
> drawbridge
> moat
> shield
> sword
> tower

Students use a 3″ x 5″ piece of paper for each word. They write and illustrate one word on each page.

After students have illustrated all the words, they arrange the papers in alphabetical order and staple them into individual booklets. They add front and back covers cut from construction paper.

These illustrated "dictionaries" come in handy at all grade levels. Use them for writing sentences, stories and reports.

FS-8307 Instant Idea Book

Say It Right

It's fun to decode messages! Through decoding your students will learn to read the pronunciation key in the dictionary.

Mysterious Messages

Write a message to your class on the chalkboard using dictionary respellings. Jokes and riddles are perfect for this!

Have students rewrite the message using the correct spellings. Students may look in a dictionary if they are unsure of a word.

Message Swap

Have students write a sentence using the pronunciation key symbols in the dictionary. Then let students exchange papers and decode the sentence.

Daily News

Write announcements for your class using dictionary respellings. Select a different student each day to read the announcement aloud.

Mēt ăt thə līˑbrĕrˑē ăfˑtər rēˑsĕs.

(Meet at the library after recess.)

nō ˈskül
tə-ˈmär-ō

Word Pictures

Your students will have fun creating word pictures.

Write a list of words on the chalkboard for students to make into word pictures. Use the list provided here and add additional words to the list that are suggested by students.

Create a picture for one or more of the words on the chalkboard, so students understand how to create word pictures.

Students select which words they want to draw as pictures. Allow students to make as many word pictures as time permits.

Post students' papers on a bulletin board for everyone to enjoy! Or, staple papers into a booklet for the classroom library.

Word Picture List
smile
nervous
jump
pop
snail
turtle
spider
see
cry
break
frown
burn
pour
push
tall
short
fat
thin
bounce
sew
swing

Adjectives Are Important

Mystery Object

This guessing game requires students to say and understand adjectives which describe an unknown object.

Gather common household objects and place each in a paper bag. Do not tell students what objects are in the bags.

Allow one student to look in a bag. That student says aloud one-word clues to describe the object. After he says each clue, he calls on students to tell what they think the object is. The first student to correctly identify the object gets to give word clues for the next object in a bag.

Each student may only make one guess about the contents of a bag. Limiting the number of responses encourages students to listen carefully to clues before using their turns.

You might want to list the clues on the chalkboard as they are announced.

A Clue a Day

Another way to play this guessing game is for you to list two clues each day on the chalkboard. On Friday just before lunch, students get to write what they think the mystery object is on slips of paper with their names. At the end of the day, read aloud the names of the students who guessed correctly. They get to leave the classroom first at dismissal time!

aquatic
wet
fast
scaly

24

Adjectives Are Important

The Five Senses

Write on the chalkboard:

> see, hear, taste, touch, smell.

Elicit from your students a list of adjectives that describe the way things appear, sound, taste, feel and smell.

Or, do the opposite and list adjectives for students to sort into correct categories.

Guess Who?

Give each student an opportunity to write adjectives to describe a classmate.

Before doing this activity, you might want to elicit a list of adjectives that describe people and jot them on the chalkboard.

Put slips of paper with students' names in an envelope. Each student draws a name. Remind students not to tell whose names they have drawn.

Every student writes a list of eight positive words or phrases to describe his chosen person.

Have students take turns reading the clues about their persons aloud. After reading the clues, a student may call on three people to guess the identity of his person.

Students love it when the teacher joins in an activity. Be certain to include your name in the drawing and to select the name of a student to write about.

Adjectives

Appearance

tall
short
thin
fat
old
young
wet
dry
round
square
dull
shiny

Sound

loud
soft
squeaky
high-pitched
low-pitched

Taste

sweet
sour
bitter
tart
spicy

Touch

bumpy
smooth
hot
cold
wet
dry
soft
hard

Smell

delicious
spicy
sweet
burnt

FS-8307 Instant Idea Book

Adjectives Are Important

This Makes Me Hungry

Before having students do this activity independently, do a group lesson. Pick a food and ask the class to help you describe it. List the clues on the chalkboard, so students understand how to write clues for food.

Students fold paper in half making two columns and label them **One** and **Two**.

Tell students to think about two of their favorite foods.

In each column students write a list of clues to describe a favorite food. They must describe the appearance, texture and taste without actually telling what the foods are.

Next, students exchange papers and try to identify the foods from the clues. Students write which food they think is being described at the top of each column. Then papers are switched back again.

This activity can be done orally. Students take turns describing their favorite foods to the class. Then they call on students to name the foods being described.

Students can also do this activity to identify animals instead of food.

ONE	TWO
green	creamy
juicy	cold
seedless	sweet
round	smooth
plump	icy
smooth	sticky
shiny	fluffy
cool	gooey

Using Adjectives and Verbs

Listing adjectives and verbs will help your students write interesting sentences.

Pictures Plus!

Every student selects a picture from a magazine of a person or an animal and pastes his picture on top of his paper.

Under his picture, the student writes adjectives to describe the animal or person. Then he writes a list of verbs that are actions that an animal or person would do.

When word lists are complete, every student writes a sentence using at least one word from each list. Older students can write several sentences or paragraphs using words from their lists.

Mike A.

white plays
furry runs
small sleeps
cute   chews
pet   eats

The furry dog plays ball.

Learning Together

This is a marvelous group lesson for grades K-1. Show the class a picture. Elicit describing words (adjectives) and action words (verbs) from the class. List the words on the chalkboard. Then ask students to dictate sentences using the words. Write the sentences on the chalkboard or on chart paper.

FS-8307   Instant Idea Book

Using Adjectives and Nouns

Pass It Along

Every student starts a sentence on his own paper and passes it to other students who add words to it. What fun to read the completed sentences after other students have added to them.

Begin by having each student write his name on a piece of paper and a sentence that begins:

A _____   _____
               describing word   noun

Next, every student passes his paper to the person in front of him. That person adds a phrase to the sentence on the paper just passed to him. The phrase he writes should tell **what** is happening. Once again every student hands the paper on which he just wrote to the person in front of him, who adds a phrase telling **where** or **when** something is happening. Finally papers are returned to the students who initially started the sentences.

Students can read their sentences aloud.

A   little   puppy   chewed my shoe   last night.
   describing   noun   what is happening   when
   word

Using Adjectives and Nouns

Colorful pictures make it easy for students to write adjectives!

Picture That . . .

Give each student a picture from a magazine that shows at least five objects. Each student should paste her picture on a piece of paper.

Have the student list five things (nouns) that are shown in her picture. Next, the student writes an adjective in front of each noun. Then students write a sentence for each of the three nouns and adjectives.

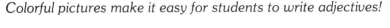

Funny Funnies

Students cut out pictures of different people and animals from magazines. They cut out the heads, pants, shoes, legs, tails, etc., from these various pictures. They rearrange the separate body parts into "funny funnies." Then students list adjectives and nouns to describe the new types of body parts on their creations.

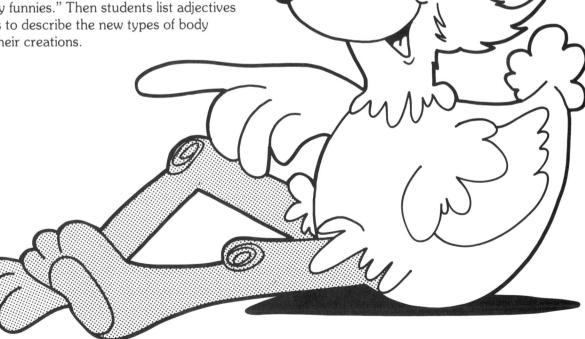

Using Words Creatively

Time for a Commercial

Give your students an opportunity to create a commercial.

Show students a few examples of advertisements that appear in magazines and newspapers. Talk about which words used in the advertisements help sell products.

Have students choose a product about which to write an ad. On drawing paper, students should draw the items they are advertising in full color.

Have students write their ads on scratch paper. Suggest that they jot down any ideas that occur to them. Next, have students select the words they want to use. Then they design their ads.

Post these advertisement posters for the whole class to enjoy.

Be an Advertising Detective

Give each student an advertisement from a magazine. Have students use red crayons to circle the adjectives that appear in their ads.

Using Words Creatively

What fun for students to write poems about themselves or their best friends!

Teach your students how to do this activity by writing a few poems together. Elicit words from the class and write a poem on the chalkboard about yourself.

Have your students follow the formula below to write their poems.

(line 1) Write your first name.

(line 2) Write two words to describe yourself.

(line 3) Write three words that name things you like to do.

(line 4) Write two more words to describe yourself.

(line 5) Write your last name.

Have students draw self-portraits to go with poems!

After students write poems about themselves, they will enjoy writing personality poems about a friend, family member, famous person or a pet.

Becky
happy, smart
reading, running, rafting
strong, kind
Greene

Very Special Greeting Cards

Have students write personality poems about their parents for Mother's Day or Father's Day cards.

FS-8307   Instant Idea Book

Using Words Creatively

A World of Colors

Ask students to think of their favorite colors. Tell students to visualize where they see those colors in our world. Then have students create poems about their favorite colors.

Each student writes her poem using the names of her favorite color as the first and last lines. Other lines begin with the color name. The poem can have as many lines as the student can create.

Example:

> Blue
> Blue is my cat's eyes.
> Blue is the sky.
> Blue is the deep ocean.
> Blue is my favorite shirt.
> Blue

Have students decorate the borders of their papers with designs in their favorite colors.

A World of Weather and Seasons

Follow the writing formula above to have students write poems about the weather or season.

Weather and Seasonal Words

fall	warm
winter	slush
spring	dry
summer	hot
day	cold
night	sleet
sun	hail
rain	morning
snow	cloudy
fog	clear
wind	humid
chilly	wet
brisk	muggy
cool	damp

Past and Present Tense

When Words

Provide practice with present and past tense forms of irregular verbs.

Have students fold lined paper in half lengthwise making two columns. Students label one column **Today** and the other **Yesterday**.

Students should number their papers from one to fifteen. Read aloud fifteen verbs, saying only the past or present tense. Students must write each verb you read aloud in the correct column.

Then have students fill in the past or present tense form for the verbs you dictated.

	TODAY	YESTERDAY
1.		
2.		
3.		
4.		
5.		
6.		
7.		
8.		
9.		
10.		
11.		

Irregular Verbs
(a partial list)

Present	Past
am	was
begin	began
blow	blew
break	broke
bring	brought
catch	caught
choose	chose
come	came
dig	dug
do	did
eat	ate
fall	fell
freeze	froze
go	went
hurt	hurt
keep	kept
know	knew
light	lit
meet	met
ride	rode
ring	rang
run	ran
sit	sat
shake	shook
sting	stung
swim	swam
take	took
tell	told
wear	wore
write	wrote

FS-8307   Instant Idea Book

Classifying Words

Cut-and-Paste Word Books

This activity is excellent for students to work on independently. It provides practice in cutting and pasting, too.

Each student folds four 9″ x 12″ pieces of construction paper like a booklet. Staple the booklets.

Have students write their names on the front covers of their booklets. They label the pages:

> hot — cold
> large — small
> work — play
> alive — not alive
> fruit — vegetable
> hard — soft

Students cut out pictures from magazines and extra workbooks to paste on the appropriate pages.

Describe It

Do this activity as a group lesson. Select a category such as fruits. Make a chart on the chalkboard or on butcher paper like the one shown below. Ask students for words which describe how each type of fruit listed, looks, feels and tastes. Or, students can work independently on individual charts.

To add to this activity, students draw a colorful illustration of each object or glue a magazine picture of each on their charts.

Other categories:
> vegetables
> beverages
> snacks
> pets
> farm animals*
> wild animals*

(*Students write words to describe how the animals look, where they live, what they eat and what they sound like.)

CATEGORY	apple	banana	cherry	orange	grape
LOOKS		long	round		silky
FEELS				bumpy	
TASTE	tart		sweet		
COLOR	red			orange	green
PICTURE	🍎		🍒	🍊	

FS-8307   Instant Idea Book

Classifying Words

Classifying words is an excellent way for students to learn vocabulary because they must think about each word's meaning.

Sounds and Textures

Write the words you want your students to learn on the chalkboard. Or, write the words on chart paper, so you have a ready-to-go lesson to use with another class.

Have students fold their papers in half to make two columns. They label one section **Feel It** and the other **Hear It**.

Have students sort out words into things they can feel (textures) or hear (sounds). Students write the words under the proper heading on their papers.

Sounds and Textures

roar	lumpy
whimper	smooth
howl	waxy
snap	bumpy
squeak	sticky
hiss	soft
rumble	gritty
bang	slick
snarl	damp
gurgle	
screech	
fizz	
moan	

Do this activity with other categories of words. *(See the list of word categories on page 9.)*

FS-8307   Instant Idea Book

Classifying Words

Two-Way Categories

These student activities can be done independently, with partners or teams. It's fun to see who can get the most words within a given time limit!

Write on the chalkboard the categories for which students must find words. Have students copy them on lined writing paper. Or, duplicate a worksheet as shown and give each student a copy.

Students write the two, three, or four categories across the tops of their papers and write the theme word(s) vertically as shown.

Give students a signal when they may begin working. After twenty minutes, have students put their pencils down. See who has the most categories correctly completed.

For variety, after a twenty-minute work period, allow students to use reference books for an additional ten minutes. Then find out who has the most correct answers.

Suggestions for theme words to write vertically:

Names of holidays: Christmas, Easter, Valentine's Day
Name of your city or state: Detroit, Michigan
Name of your school: Johnston Elementary
Names of famous persons: Washington, Stowe
Names of seasons: spring, summer, fall, winter
Phrases: Spring Is Here, Summer Fun

NAME Barbara
category words:

	birds	fruit	spice
M	martin	melon	mint
I			
C	canary		cumin
H			
I			
G		grapes	
A			anise
N			nutmeg

Categories for Classification

names of cities	animals
names of states	girls' names
names of countries	boys' names
names of U.S. Presidents	colors
pieces of clothing	vegetables
names of trees	fruits
names of flowers	sports
insects	occupations
kinds of dogs	types of transportation
jungle animals	foods
farm animals	spices
	musical instruments

Classifying Words

Let's Play Categories

Write a category on the chalkboard. For example: a color word. *(A category list appears on page 36.)*

Set a timer for three minutes. Tell students to list as many color words as they can think of in three minutes.

When the time limit expires, ask students to count the words on their lists. Have the student with the longest list read her color words aloud.

For variety, or with younger students, do this as a group brainstorming activity. Have students name color words. Jot the words on the chalkboard. See how many the class can come up with in three minutes.

a color word:

orange

purple

blue

YELLOW

Word Collection

Elicit a category of words from your students and jot them on a strip of butcher paper or chart paper. Post this word chart. Tell students to continue to hunt for more words for the chart. When students suggest additional words, add them to the list.

robin
dove
finch
cardinal
chickadee

Alphabet Word-o!

Can your students think of a word for every letter of the alphabet?

Give each student a strip of paper. Have students print the alphabet vertically on their papers.

Tell students to write a word beside each letter.

After everyone has written as many words as he can think of independently, share words orally so all students will have a word for each letter.

Have students illustrate as many words as possible on their lists.

Do this activity independently or with partners.

e
f
g
h

elephant
fish
gate
hat

Color Word-o Booklets

Give each student a booklet of construction paper pages. Students write the names of objects that are yellow on the yellow page in their booklets, the names of blue objects on the blue page, and so on.

Or, use strips of butcher paper in different colors to do this as a group activity. Elicit words from the class and write them on the appropriate color of paper. When students think of additional words, add them to the lists.

lemon drop
sun
daffodils
lemons
buttercups
egg yolks
pencils

butter
chicks
squash
mustard

Developing Sentences

Add-a-Word

Have students add their own words to the sentence formats you write on the board. Give students an opportunity to hear some sentences written by other students.

Write these sentences on the board. Draw a line to indicate where students need to provide a word. Students must copy the sentences and supply missing words.

That _____ cat is _____ .

The _____ dog barked _____ _____ _____ .

The _____ man laughed _____ _____ _____ .

Look at that _____ balloon _____ _____ _____ .

Tell students to each choose one sentence to illustrate. Have students read aloud the sentences they illustrated.

Look at that <u>huge</u> balloon <u>rising</u> <u>above</u> <u>us.</u>

Create a Worksheet

Have students write three sentences which are missing adjectives or phrases. Students swap papers with partners and fill in the missing words.

Crazy Clusters

Students weave unrelated words into sentences or stories. Write groups of unrelated words on the chalkboard: elephant, drainpipe, stars; recess, tunnel, turkey. Each student chooses a group of words and writes a sentence using all three words. Have every student illustrate the completed sentence.

The elephant slid down the drainpipe under the stars!

Who Said That?

Write a list of words on the chalkboard that can be substituted for the word "said."

Substitutes for "Said"

yelled	promised
asked	answered
whispered	concluded
pleaded	announced
declared	hinted
cried	bellowed
called	shouted
bragged	blurted
argued	stated
admitted	mentioned
insisted	recited

Students must select three words from the list and write a sentence for each word.

Cartoon Quips

Ask students to cut single-frame cartoons from newspapers. Provide a box or bag where students can deposit the cartoons they gather. Cut and discard the captions from the cartoons and give each student two cartoons. Students paste the cartoons on their papers and write new captions. Students' papers can be compiled into a booklet and added to the classroom library.

FS-8307   Instant Idea Book

Key Words and Phrases

Twosies and Threesies

Write a list of commonly used two- and three-word phrases on the chalkboard.

Ask students to fill in the missing words for these "twosies" and "threesies."

Twosies:

cup and _____ (saucer)
salt and _____ (pepper)
bread and _____ (butter)
now or _____ (never)
hearts and _____ (flowers)
hide and _____ (seek)
high and _____ (dry/low)
night and _____ (day)
cats and _____ (dogs)

up and _____ (down)
cops and _____ (robbers)
cut and _____ (paste)
huff and _____ (puff)
peace and _____ (quiet)
toss and _____ (turn)
sticks and _____ (stones)
lost and _____ (found)
pins and _____ (needles)

Threesies:

red, white and _____ (blue)
snap, crackle and _____ (pop)
tall, dark and _____ (handsome)
hop, skip, and a _____ (jump)
reading, writing and _____ (arithmetic)
bacon, lettuce and _____ (tomato)
up, up and _____ (away)

FS-8307   Instant Idea Book

Key Words and Phrases

What's Missing?

Students must supply a word to complete each common expression below. Write the phrases on the chalkboard.

Common Expressions

a bag of _____
a bar of _____
a basket of _____
a bucket of _____
a stick of _____
a tube of _____
a plate of _____
a slice of _____
a bottle of _____
a bowl of _____
a box of _____
a carton of _____
a cup of _____
a piece of _____
a jar of _____

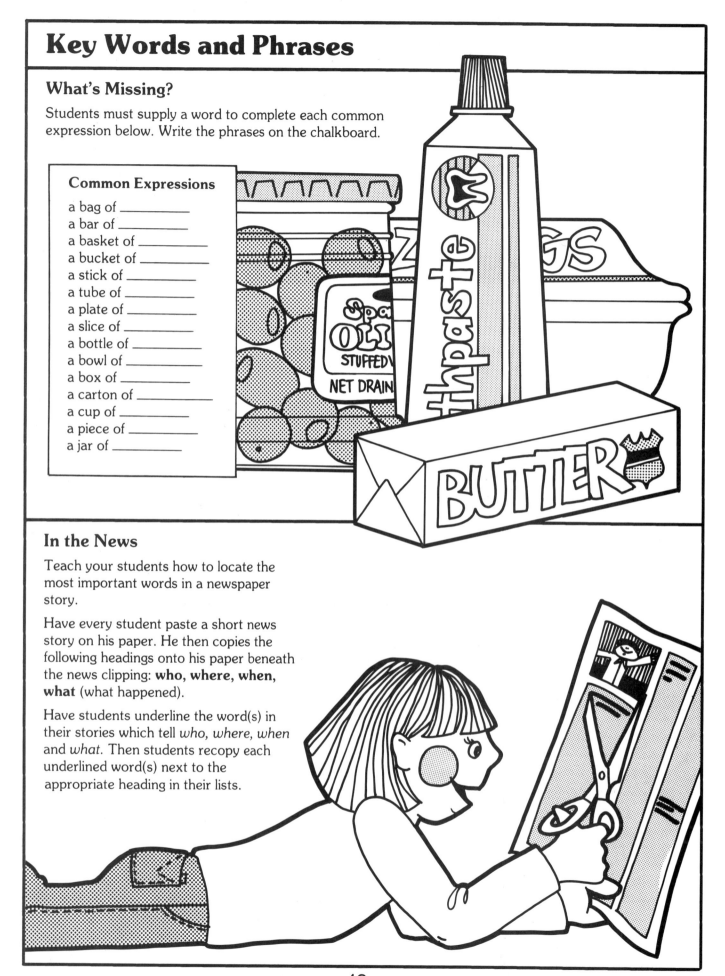

In the News

Teach your students how to locate the most important words in a newspaper story.

Have every student paste a short news story on his paper. He then copies the following headings onto his paper beneath the news clipping: **who, where, when, what** (what happened).

Have students underline the word(s) in their stories which tell *who, where, when* and *what*. Then students recopy each underlined word(s) next to the appropriate heading in their lists.

FS-8307   Instant Idea Book

Similes

Show your students how to add interest and details to their writing by using similes.

Print unfinished similes on the chalkboard, a reusable tagboard chart, or a duplicating master.

Similes

as light as a _____

as cold as _____

as cute as _____

as soft as _____

as hard as _____

as clear as _____

as bright as _____

as dark as _____

as green as _____

as strong as _____

as busy as a _____

as quick as _____

as stubborn as _____

as deep as _____

as rough as _____

as white as _____

worked like _____

sparkled like _____

brown like _____

sang like _____

swam like _____

tall like _____

slow like _____

ran like _____

round like _____

jumped like _____

crawled like _____

blue like _____

short like _____

tasted like _____

sounded like _____

sweet like _____

Students must add a word or phrase to complete each simile.

   FS-8307   Instant Idea Book

Terrific Tongue Twisters

Tongue twisters are fun to write, read and recite.

Most students are familiar with the favorite tongue twister about Peter Piper. (*Peter Piper picked a peck of pickled peppers.*)

List some tongue-twister starters on the chalkboard.

Tongue Twister Starters

Wally Walrus
Henrietta Hippo
Abigail Alligator
Perky Pig
Ladybug Lilly
Boopsie Butterfly
Goofy Gorilla
Tiny Turtle
Zingy Zebra
Slinky Snake
Hugo Horse
Tango Tiger
Buzzy Bumblebee
Katie Kangaroo

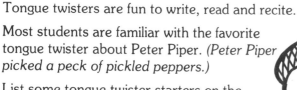

Tell each student to write a one-line tongue-twister sentence. Students must begin their sentences with one of the twister starters from the chalkboard. Each word must start with the same letter, but students can also use these words: *to, a, an, the, in, of, by, for, near.*

After students have written their tongue-twisters, they can draw pictures to illustrate their sentences. Older students can write additional lines for their tongue twisters.

Abigail Alligator always asks for apples, acorns or ants in autumn.

Basal Reader Activities

Basal reader stories are an excellent source for vocabulary development activities.

It's As Easy As One, Two, Three

Students practice counting syllables with this word hunt activity. Use the basal reader, so no one needs spelling help.

Students fold their papers into three columns and label their columns **One, Two,** and **Three.** They list words from their basal readers with one, two or three syllables under the appropriate column. To make this more difficult, students can add a fourth column to their papers.

ONE TWO T

FS-8307 Instant Idea Book

Basal Reader Activities

Very Important People

Students improve their vocabulary and skimming skills with this lesson.

Have students divide their papers into three sections. They label the sections: **Who, Feeling,** and **Page Number**.

Students skim through stories they have already read in their basal readers. Each person lists the name of a character in a story and writes a word to describe the way that character felt at a certain point in the story. Then the student writes the page number to indicate where in the story the character felt that way.

For example:

Who	Feeling	Page Number
Beth	*surprised*	*42*

Have students list three or more characters, feelings, and page numbers.

To make this more difficult, add a fourth reading heading—**Evidence**. Have students write what the character did in the story to show that he or she had that feeling.

For example:

Who	Feeling	Evidence	Page Number
Beth	*surprised*	*she screamed*	*42*

   FS-8307   Instant Idea Book

Basal Reader Activities

Hard or Soft?

This activity provides practice with hard and soft **c** and **g** sounds. Students may work independently or with a partner.

Have students fold their papers two times, so there are four sections. They label the sections:

soft **g**
hard **g**
soft **c**
hard **c**

Have students skim through stories to find words to list inside each of these sections.

Story Skimmer

See which students can come up with the most words in each category by having them skim through a story in the basal reader.

Students fold their papers into three sections. Label the sections: **Size, When,** and **Where.**

As students skim through the story, they find words that refer to size, when and where. Students write the words in the appropriate sections on their papers. (Set a reasonable time limit for your students.)

When time is up, find out who has the most words in each category. Have that student read her words aloud.

Basal Reader Activities

On Location

Combine basal reading with a special activity about the setting of a story.

Have students look through their basal readers at the last three stories they read. Each student should choose one location mentioned in one of the stories.

Students make lists of descriptive phrases and words used in the story about this location. Then each student writes three sentences to describe the setting in his own words. Finally, he draws a picture of the story setting he chose.

spooky
deserted
old
creaky

Count to Ten

Students number their papers from one to ten. Tell students that they must find a word with one letter to write next to the number one, a word with two letters to write next to the number two and so on. Signal students to begin.

Students see how many words they can get in six minutes. Words must be spelled correctly. When their time is up, share answers, so all have a word written by each number.

WRITE RIGHT

one	a
two	in
three	egg
four	gate
five	count
six	school
seven	support
eight	flourish
nine	encourage
ten	themselves

Basal Reader Activities

Vocabulary Bingo

Students search through the basal reader for words to write in the bingo grid boxes.

(Reproduce the bingo grid on page 50.)

Tell students they must find a word in their basal readers for each box. The same word may not be used in more than one box.

The first student to fill in every box is the winner! All words must be spelled correctly.

Ready, Set, Words!

Write a title from a basal reader story on the chalkboard. Direct students to list as many words as they can using only the letters from the title. Set an appropriate time limit.

At the end of the time limit, students count the number of words they wrote. Each student writes her total at the top of her paper and circles it. Award stickers to the top ten students—those with the highest number of correct words.

FS-8307 Instant Idea Book

Vocabulary Bingo

Write a word in each box below.

one syllable _____	soft **c** _____	add —**ing** _____	ends with —**sh** _____
compound _____	add —**s** _____	a place _____	soft **g** _____
ends with —**ch** _____	add —**est** _____	two syllables _____	add —**ed** _____
an action _____	contraction _____	a feeling _____	hard **c** _____
add —**er** _____	add —**es** _____	hard **g** _____	three syllables _____

Illustrated Idioms

Help students understand idiomatic expressions with this high-interest lesson.

Write a list of idioms on the chalkboard. Discuss the meaning of some of these expressions. To save time, print the idioms on a piece of chart paper to use again with another activity or class.

Assign each student a different idiomatic expression. Each student draws an illustration to show the literal meaning of his expression. Students should print the expressions below their illustrations.

Post the illustrated idioms on a bulletin board or staple into a booklet for the classroom library.

Students benefit from seeing examples of other students' work. Save samples to use as teaching tools with future classes.

Idioms
full of baloney
half-hearted
fell head over heels
burned her bridges behind her
go fly a kite
cold feet
pulling my leg
laughed his head off
see through someone
on pins and needles
down in the dumps
chip off the old block
raining cats and dogs
let the cat out of the bag
spoiled rotten
under the weather
all thumbs
like two peas in a pod
walking on air
filled with hot air
turn over a new leaf
speak up
worth her weight in gold
heavy-hearted
feeling his oats
fell for it
tightfisted
hit the roof
drive him up the wall

FS-8307   Instant Idea Book

Survival Words

Help students learn to read and understand words that appear on highway signs.

Read That Sign

Make a few replicas of road signs from construction paper.
For example:

Ask students to explain the meaning of the road signs. Discuss the correct meaning of each sign with the class. Display the signs on a bulletin board.

Tell students to watch for additional signs. Students can make sketches of the signs they see and bring their sketches to school.

When a student brings a sketch of a road sign, that student creates her own replica on construction paper for the bulletin board. Discuss the meaning of each new sign as it is added to the display.

Important Words to Learn

Make flashcards or posters of informational and warning signs. Use the list of survival words.

Survival Words
Exit
Entrance
No Trespassing
Do Not Enter
Poison
Emergency
Danger
Flammable
Out of Order
Fire Exit
Detour
Railroad Crossing
Restrooms
Private
Hospital
Keep Out
Caution
Be Careful
Information
Signal Ahead
One Way
Wet Paint
Doctor
External Use Only

Vocabulary Expansion

Animal Babies

Help your students expand their vocabularies by learning the correct names for animal offspring.

Write a list of animals on the chalkboard. In a separate word box on the chalkboard, write the names of the offspring of the animals in a different order than your chalkboard list.

Tell students they must try to write the name of each animal's offspring in parentheses after the name of the adult animal.

Share answers orally to make sure everyone has the correct answers.

Have each student draw and label an illustration of one animal with its offspring.

Animal Offspring

horse (foal)	cow (calf)
sheep (lamb)	dog (puppy)
bear (cub)	goose (gosling)
whale (calf)	swan (cygnet)
kangaroo (joey)	beaver (kit)
cat (kitten)	chicken (chick)
deer (fawn)	eel (elver)
goat (kid)	lion (cub)
rabbit (bunny)	pig (piglet)
seal (pup)	turkey (poult)

Older students can list titles of books and the characters within the stories which personify these animals.

Charlotte's Web—Wilbur, pig
Bambi—Bambi, fawn
            Thumper, rabbit

FS-8307   Instant Idea Book

Vocabulary Expansion

Help students learn the correct names for groups of animals.

A Group of Animals

List phrases on the board like "a _____ of bees" or "a _____ of cows." In a separate word box, write the various animals' group names in a different order than they appear in the list.

Have students number their papers and write the missing animal's group name by each number. Or, you can write an incorrect word for the animal group and have students rearrange the words correctly.

For example:
> a herd of fish
> a school of geese
> a flock of cows

Share answers orally to make sure everyone has the correct answers.

Have students make color illustrations of groups of animals and label them.

Animal Groups

swarm of bees
herd of cows
troop of monkeys
colony of rabbits
pod of seals
pack of dogs
school of fish
gaggle or flock of geese
pride of lions
gam or pod of whales

Can Animals Think?

Everyone likes animals. Students will have fun drawing scenes to show what animals are saying and thinking!

Students draw scenes that include several animals. Every student adds conversation balloons (as in a cartoon strip) and writes what the animals are saying or thinking.

I wonder if I'll get warts if I touch a person?

Vocabulary Expansion

Happy Homonyms

Your students will learn about homonyms and make a fun-to-read book for the classroom library at the same time!

Write a list of homonyms on the chalkboard. Assign each student a pair of homonyms to illustrate. (Jot the student's name or initials beside the pair of homonyms he is responsible for illustrating, so you know which homonyms have been assigned.)

Post illustrated homonyms on a bulletin board or staple the illustrations together into a booklet for the classroom library.

Select a student to decorate the cover of the homonym booklet.

Save the homonym booklet until next year to use again when you are teaching homonyms.

Older students can create and illustrate mixed-up homonym phrases like:

fur tree	hare-raising story
weather vein	tall tail
yard sail	read nose
deer friend	see serpent

Homonyms

prints — prince
hair — hare
doe — dough
horse — hoarse
pail — pale
sun — son
flower — flour
stair — stare
road — rode
wail — whale
aunt — ant
sea — see
mail — male
beat — beet
blew — blue
flew — flu
fir — fur
week — weak
cent — scent
tail — tale
vein — vane
rain — rein
meet — meat
dear — deer
ate — eight
break — brake
sail — sale
heal — heel
read — red
no — know
die — dye
plane — plain
one — won
hymn — him

Vocabulary Expansion

Multiple Meanings

Explain to your class that homographs are words that are spelled alike but have different meanings or pronunciations.

Write homographs on the chalkboard. Discuss the multiple meanings of several homographs. Write two sentences for one of the homographs to further illustrate the concept. For example:

> Where did you *park* the car?
> We have a picnic in the *park*.

Assign each student a homograph. Every student writes two sentences to show the multiple meanings of his word.

Allow several students to read their pairs of sentences aloud.

Homographs

bill
pound
pupil
chest
cold
soil
pitcher
punch
stamp
saw
watch
roll
drop
pet
tire
seal
stand
nail
pick
trip
spring
fall
line
tip
sink
bat
duck
play
pool
wave
yard
ring

FS-8307 Instant Idea Book

Vocabulary Expansion

Help your students understand proverbs with these high-interest activities.

Proverbs

Discuss the meaning of one specific proverb with your students. Then write unfinished proverbs on the chalkboard for your students to copy and complete with imaginative endings of their own. For example: Let sleeping dogs . . . .

             Haste makes . . . .

             Don't count your chickens . . . .

Have students read aloud a few of the proverbs they wrote. After students have finished writing, you may want to complete each proverb with its traditional ending on the chalkboard.

Act It Out

Divide students into small groups. Have each group act out a proverb and ask the class to figure out which proverb is being pantomimed.

Think About It

Have each student interpret a proverb. Every student writes a proverb on paper then explains what he thinks the proverb means. Students read their interpretations and the class discusses other possible meanings. Or, instead of writing their interpretations, students have an oral discussion. Have one student speak in support of a particular interpretation and call on another person to explain a different message in the proverb.

Proverbs

Better late than never.
Look before you leap.
Don't cry over spilled milk.
Haste makes waste.
Don't count your chickens before they're hatched.
He who hesitates is lost.
Birds of a feather flock together.
If at first you don't succeed, try, try again.
Two heads are better than one.
Let sleeping dogs lie.
Better safe than sorry.
Actions speak louder than words.
Easy come, easy go.
A bird in the hand is worth two in the bush.
Nothing ventured, nothing gained.
He who laughs last, laughs best.
A rolling stone gathers no moss.

     FS-8307   Instant Idea Book

Reproducible Pages

Name: _____

Words to Study

1. _____
2. _____
3. _____
4. _____
5. _____
6. _____
7. _____
8. _____
9. _____
10. _____
11. _____
12. _____

Name: _____

My Word List

1. _____
2. _____
3. _____
4. _____
5. _____

Name: _____

Important Words!

1. _____
2. _____
3. _____
4. _____
5. _____

a reproducible page
FS-8307   Instant Idea Book

My Flashcards

A Word Wheel

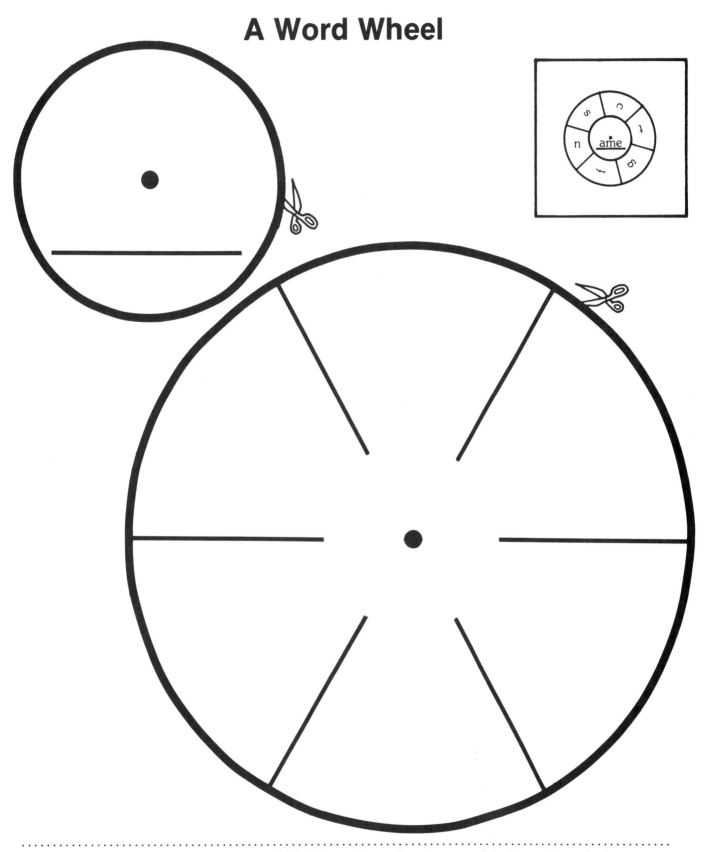

Teacher: Have students cut out the circles. Each child places the small circle on top of the large circle and pokes a fastener through the centers of both circles. Every child writes a word family on the line in the small circle and prints one letter inside each space in the large circle to form different words with the word family. Children read their words aloud as they turn their word wheels.

©Frank Schaffer Publications, Inc.   61   FS-8307 Instant Idea Book
a reproducible page

Learning Words

Teacher: To make tachistoscopes have students write a word on each line on their paper strips. Each student cuts out the strip along the dotted lines, cuts two slits inside animal picture, and pulls the paper strip with words through the slits. Students may cut out other paper strips to learn different words.

CONGRATULATIONS

TO

_____

**A
Real Word Wizard**

_____
Teacher Signature

_____
Date

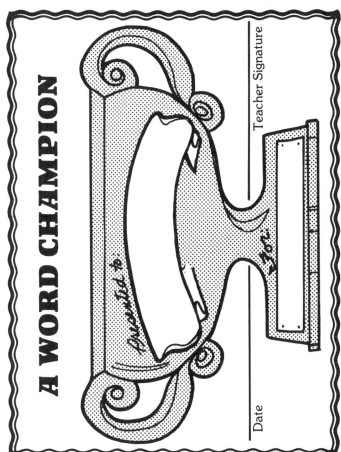

A WORD CHAMPION

Presented to

Teacher Signature

Date

_____
Student Name

HAS
WORD POWER!

_____
Teacher Signature

_____
Date

Announcing
A SUPER-DUPER
WORD WONDER!

Awarded to: _____

Teacher: _____

Date: _____

FS-8307   Instant Idea Book